Finding Happiness

In Faith, Family & Work

Also from Boys Town Press

Boys Town: A Photographic History

*Letters from the Front: Boys Town on the Battlefield
from Pearl Harbor to the Persian Gulf*

*The Ongoing Journey: Awakening Spiritual Life
in At-Risk Youth*

Dreams Fulfilled: Success Stories from Boys Town

Common Sense Parenting

Finding Happiness
In Faith, Family & Work

Words of Practical Irish Wisdom from Father Flanagan

BOYS TOWN, NEBRASKA

Publisher's Cataloging-in-Publication
(Provided by Quality Books, Inc.)

Flanagan, Edward Joseph, 1886-1948.
    Finding happiness in faith, family and work : words of
practical Irish wisdom / from Father Flanagan ; [edited by
Barbara A. Lonnborg].
    p. cm.
    ISBN: 1-889322-00-8

    1. Flanagan, Edward Joseph, 1886-1948--Quotations. 2. Youth-
Quotations, maxims, etc. 3. Family--Quotations, maxims, etc. 4.
Character--Quotations, maxims, etc. 5. Work--Quotations,
maxims, etc. 6. Success--Quotations, maxims, etc. 7. Faith-
Quotations, maxims, etc. 8. Spiritual life--Quotations, maxims,
etc. I. Lonnborg, Barbara. II. Title.

HQ796.F53 1997   305.23'5
                                    QBI97-40262

Boys Town Press
14100 Crawford Rd.
Boys Town, Nebraska 68010
www.ffbh.boystown.org
1-800-282-6657

Table of Contents

Father Flanagan's Legacy

At the time of his death in 1948, Father Edward J. Flanagan was in Germany on a fact-finding mission for the U.S. War Department on the plight of orphaned children. He was known and revered worldwide.

Father Flanagan consulted with presidents, governors, and generals on issues of youth and family. His work with homeless boys and the founding of Boys Town had been celebrated on film in an Oscar-winning performance by Spencer Tracy. Replicas of his Nebraska home for abandoned boys sprang up in countries around the world. He spoke often before national civic and social organizations and addressed millions more in his weekly *Links of Love* radio program.

In a voice that still carried the cadence of County Roscommon, his Irish birthplace, Father Flanagan spoke passionately about the needs of children, the importance of faith and family, the value of hard work, the components of character, the rewards of sacrifice, and the measurement of happiness and success. These beliefs had been forged first before the Flanagan hearth in rural Ireland while growing up with ten brothers and sisters and later reinforced during his thirty years of work giving a home to hundreds of boys who had lost theirs through violence, illness, or poverty.

From 1918 to 1948, Father Flanagan shared his thoughts on these themes many times in his monthly and bimonthly columns written for the *Father Flanagan's Boys' Home Journal* and the *Boys Town Times*, now archived in the Boys Town Hall of History. The reflections in this book are excerpted from those columns and his many speeches.

His voice has been stilled for half a century, but Father Flanagan's words resonate with truth and power for us today.

Youth Today
& Tomorrow

A young person should never be made to feel

that no great thing is expected of him or her.

I have faith in American boys and girls.
I say there is no such thing as a bad boy; the same
applies to our girls. A boy or girl given the proper
guidance and direction, kept busy and constructively
occupied, will prove my statement.

The child may be given every material advantage and still not have the feeling that he is secure in his environment. This comes from consciousness of being wanted. It is the awareness that someone cares. It is a certain confidence the child has because of the attitude of others toward him. It is the feeling that he belongs, that he is accepted, because of the contribution he makes toward the needs and happiness of the group.

Youth needs the force of good and attractive examples. Children are not philosophers, but they are apt imitators. They may be easily led to follow where they cannot be driven.

We take stock of everything else. Why not take
stock of our greatest assets, our boys and girls?
It is a wise community which . . . sets about solving
its youth problems. Truly, with respect to youth,
an ounce of prevention is worth a pound of cure.
The task may appear difficult, but it is not impossible.
It can, in fact, it has been done.

Finding fault with the boy, criticizing him, and
constantly reminding him at home of his mistakes
will never improve his condition. But if you encourage
him, praising him for the little signs of improvement
you see in him, he will soon begin to think he is not so
bad after all, and it will give him greater incentive
to try harder and harder.

The poor, innocent, unfortunate little children belong

to us, and it is our problem to give them every chance

to develop into good men and women. This must

be done before the marks of neglect become

too deeply embedded in their little minds and hearts,

and the habits of crime and vice make their wills

impotent to function and to respond to kindness and

love administered too late.

Let us not forget children always seek the good will, praise and love of others, and nothing is so certain to kill and destroy their ambition and spirit as fault-finding and scolding.

If we are to build citizens of tomorrow, we must
emphasize today the importance of proper incentive,
of wholesome recreation, of sympathetic guidance
and helpful environment.

The child who has learned to think and act
constructively has already been given an important
start to success and happiness.

When you help a child today,

you write the history of tomorrow.

Who knows but that some future benefactor
of mankind is now a homeless orphan, sleeping
in alleys, eating such food as he can find, and waiting
only for some understanding person to take him
and start him on the way to real achievement.

Our young people are our greatest asset.
Give them a chance, and they will give a good
account of themselves.

There are no bad boys. There is only bad environment,

bad training, bad example, bad thinking.

It has always been a source of great satisfaction to me
to watch a child acquire strength and dignity
of character. Children acquire character through their
desire to emulate and practice the principles of right
living laid before them by those they love and respect.

Keep our youth busy; keep them occupied.

Let us all work together and not let our youth down.

They need guidance, supervision, and religious training.

Youth is a time of dreams, of high aspirations and enthusiasm. Criticism, neglect, and indifference have a withering effect on the spirit of the growing boy or girl. They take out of them the zest of life which God put under their ribs.

The boy goes where his father goes. He does what his father does, not what his father says he should do.

Youth who have not been loved and protected are not likely to love others and protect the rights of others.

Often it has been said that youth is the nation's greatest asset. But it is more than that – it is the world's greatest asset. More than that, it is perhaps the world's only hope.

Family Life
& the Home

Let us attend to first things first – our God-given duties.

Parenthood is the most sacred office, endowed

with the highest responsible duties ever given

to man and woman.

The home is the oldest established unit in human society. When the home fails, a small but a vital part of the community fails. It becomes a danger point of infection for the whole community, and the whole community, in some measure becomes affected by the failure.

The family background could solve many
a social problem which today is most perplexing
to the sincere social worker.

Parents stand on a pinnacle of honor in society, and in their hands are the precious souls of their loved ones to be formed and shaped into types that will meet with the wish of the Creator.

Isn't sacrifice the real measure of love? Genuine love in married life comes only to two people who are mutually and supremely unselfish.

For the benefit of discouraged parents who have been trying so hard to do their duty as they know it toward their children: As long as you can keep the confidence of your children, you need have no fear. Approach the subject of their weakness with understanding and sympathy. Never lose your patience with such a child. Remember the child has faith in you. Perhaps you are the only one he or she would come to in difficulty, and you must not shut out the last ray of hope.

When discipline is lax, or when it is applied

in a haphazard manner so that the child doesn't know

what to expect, parental authority breaks down

and the child's mind is thrown into a state

of chaotic confusion.

The home should be a sanctuary of love . . . a place

where people live, where the cares and worries

of the office are forgotten, where the laughter

of children is heard, where one can find time

for companionship and meditation.

Parents do not fail because they want to fail.

They fail because they don't want to succeed.

They are indifferent. They expect the school

and the church to do their job for them.

Parents should be prudent in teaching their children,
and explaining to them very early in life, that it is not
a good thing to receive everything they want or desire.

What goal have you won when you attain even
the loftiest success if respect and love do not exist
between you and your sons and daughters?

Social living must be learned by children
if they are to lead social lives. Where the home fails,
some other means must be used. Where the training
is utterly neglected, the social order fails, and the
whole social order must pay for the neglect.
We pay in taxes, in trouble, in labor, and saddest of all,
we pay in broken hearts.

Constant criticism is often the result of impatience in adults rather than imperfection in children. Criticism should be constructive and given in a spirit of encouragement. Criticism should be tempered with praise.

No man or woman can deem himself or herself
a success in life, no matter how far up the ladder they
have climbed, either socially, mentally or materially,
if they cannot say that they have the confidence,
comradeship, and the love of their children.

Work, Discipline
& Character

We need those who in fulfillment of their dreams,

will risk hardships and who are prepared

to be jeered at, yet who will carry on in spite

of everything to prove their conviction.

There is something lacking in the kind of education which teaches a youth how to make a living, but which does not teach him or her how to make a life. I do not want to minimize the importance of making a living. We must eat. We must have clothes to wear. We do need to have a roof over our heads. But there is a vast difference between living to eat and eating to live.

A life without discipline is like a ship without a rudder. It is subjected to every whim. Contentment comes from knowing what to do and in doing it.

To teach young children occasionally to perform their duty is of little avail. Loose stones scattered all over a field no more build a house than do stray acts of duty make a dutiful person. We must teach our children to grow into doing their duty unconsciously or automatically, just as an athlete performing difficult feats with ease and grace.

There is wisdom in the habit of looking

at the bright side of life.

The successful person, the person who has made happy adjustments to his environment, is the person who has developed the right kind of habits.

The feeling of importance should spring

from living importantly.

My idea of a good citizen is a useful citizen. He must be good, but he must be good for something. He must be willing to give others the same latitude he demands for himself respecting individual rights and privileges.

No boy's education is complete until he has been
taught to accept nothing from life except what
he can win with his own hands. We all must work.
We all have some job to do.

The ability to help oneself is important in the struggle
between the individual and the environment.
That is how character is made. The sinews of character
are hardened by each victory we win.

Some of the finest people in the world go through life

under a handicap because they never learned how

to play when they were children.

The value we put on anything is revealed

by what we are willing to sacrifice to possess it.

The man or woman who succeeds in life today
or at any time must necessarily be a man or woman
of strong character who will not falter or succumb
to every obstacle that comes up.

Academic education is entirely pointless if it does not build character. The best and most complete education teaches the art of living, and social living without character is frankly impossible.

There is a silent dignity, a fundamental usefulness,

a primeval necessity in work.

Attitudes can be, and often are, far more important than abilities in shaping the individual for success or failure.

No one is too good to perform

whatever is required of him.

The measure of a man is determined

by the way he reacts to his environment.

Every child is better off for earning at least part
of what he or she spends. It is a parent's responsibility
to teach a child to be thrifty, to pay his or her own way,
and still be willing to share with those in need.

Having a definite purpose or aim makes it possible for us to live more fully in the present. Only by doing the task immediately before us are we able to reach our objective. The person who dwells in the past, like the person who lives too much in the future gets little done. He misses the significance of the present.

Character is formed by doing the thing
we are supposed to do, when it should be done,
whether we feel like doing it or not.

The higher the ideal the more work is required to accomplish it. Do not expect to become a great success in life if you are not willing to work for it.

The law of life is the law of work. Parents should teach their children the importance of doing. Work teaches appreciation. It creates a sense of responsibility. It builds morale through the satisfaction of achievement.

Achievement is the meter of growth, and we must grow mentally and spiritually as well as in years.

It is a work-a-day world into which our youngsters
are born, and there will always be work to do.
The keenest satisfaction they will ever achieve
will come from tasks well accomplished, obstacles
overcome, and goals achieved.

Happiness &
Success in Life

Happiness is an important factor in successful living, but happiness comes from appreciating the things we have, not from the mere possession of them. Our greatest problems come from within rather than from without, and by the same token, the wise person is he who carries his wealth with him, who has learned the value of appreciation.

Gratitude is the flower in the wilderness,

the leavening of life, and the song amidst sorrows.

Many individuals lack any definite purpose. They are not quite sure what they want. They live from day to day, doing the best they can under the circumstances, but lacking a consuming ambition, they never seem to get anywhere.

What we are or hope to become is revealed by the values we cherish. Value is the wellspring of action. To value is to desire, to desire is to strive, and to strive is to become.

More important than wealth and position
in the determination of individual happiness are
good manners. They are recognized and accepted
by good people everywhere. They give a person
poise and dignity. They are evidence of real worth.

The person who lacks purpose makes a good follower,
but a poor leader. The leader is one who has
an objective. By virtue of strength of purpose, he or she
commands the respect and following of others
who may be equally intelligent and gifted, but who
do not have the power of will to make the most
of their endowments.

To be the kind of person God intended one to be is the crowning achievement of right living. Get an education, get friends, get a worthwhile goal to strive for – but first get character, for character is the foundation upon which the superstructure of a successful life is built.

Success is a question of degrees, not of completion.
The most successful men and women, the men and
women who have accomplished much with their lives,
are precisely the ones who never seem able to
catch up with their ambitions.

Thoughtfulness of others helps make others thoughtful of us. It generates good feeling. It invites friendships which pave the way for future opportunities.

The person who lacks purpose

will never go far or do much.

For successful people, aspiration is as important as inspiration is. The joy and satisfaction they get come from living rather than from life. They know that it is only when a person gives up, content to live in the past instead of in the future, that the heart grows weary.

Just as the way to have friends is to be a friend,

so too the way to win respect is to show respect.

Lack of gratitude has caused more heartaches, more
sorrow, than perhaps any other failing in our nature.
It has turned an aged father's or mother's hair white
and sent them heartbroken to the grave; it has
deprived friendships of their sweetest understandings;
and it has robbed many a generous-hearted
man or woman of faith in mankind.

Although enthusiasm is a characteristic of youth, it does not follow that enthusiasm belongs to the young alone. I have known men advanced in years, but in whose eyes could still be seen the sparkle of youth. And I have known boys who have been pushed around and neglected, boys who have been abandoned and left to filch food from garbage cans and sleep in the alleys, and in their eyes I have seen the furtive look of defeat.

Perhaps the most remarkable characteristic of the successful man is his singleness of purpose. He does not scatter his efforts. He has one primary objective. Nothing is allowed to stand in the way of its achievement.

The foundation for successful living must be laid early. In building a life, as in building a house, we first must have something to build on. It is not essential to a child to have material advantages and comforts, but that a child have a sense of true values, constructive habits, and a wholesome attitude toward life.

Good manners are more than a sign of good breeding; they are an asset to every person who aspires for social advantage or business success.

Faith, Hope
& Charity

Without God at the beginning,

there can only be confusion at the end.

The fact is that nothing earthly

can fill the void in the human heart.

Without religious faith there can be no lasting
enthusiasm. Man cannot lift himself by tugging
at his own bootstraps.

If there is in the Gospel a positive or fundamental law,
it is certainly the law of charity. The outstanding
Christian character, therefore, will be known by . . . love
of his neighbor. Let the spirit of love permeate all
your actions with your fellow man.

You and I must pray. We must pray unceasingly, perseveringly. Our homes must become sanctuaries of prayer. We must grow strong through prayer and sacrifice.

Successful teaching calls for more than a knowledge
of textbooks; it calls for an understanding of life,
for an appreciation of human values.

I see no disaster threatening us because of any particular race, creed or color. But I do see danger for all in an ideology which discriminates against anyone politically or economically because he or she was born into the 'wrong' race, has skin of the 'wrong' color, or worships at the 'wrong' altar.

If we want to live in a good world, then we must help make it that kind of world by our acts and prayers. If we want good will to reign, then we must see first that we are people of good will.

I like to think of music as being the language
of the soul. It reveals to us truth and beauty beyond
the power of words to describe. Music goes beyond
the barriers of race, creed, or geography. It is a
spiritual medium of mutual fellowship for all people –
for the rich and the poor, for the mighty and the meek,
for the old and for the young.

No greater act of charity could be done

than helping a homeless child.

A good deed lives forever, a lasting monument to your memory which will endure long after you are gone.

We sometimes forget that without happiness there is no such thing as success, and no one can be truly happy unless he or she is of service to others.

Every act of courtesy is a recognition of the rights

of the person to whom courtesy is shown.

Faith and work make a triumphant combination.

No motive for good lives can exceed religion
in its power. God and God alone in the lives of fathers
and mothers, boys and girls, can best teach the laws
of right and social living. The well being of society
and of the individuals who compose it, depends
upon their observance.

What sadder fate is there for any human being than
to be left alone, forsaken, without a friend, to sink down
into the cesspool of vice and sin, all for the want
of a little charity?

In the happiness brought to others,

our own happiness is reflected.

Christian charity does not consist in the shedding of tears, or in mere preaching, but rather in the doing of that which we preach, and in the actual alleviation of the conditions that bring about those tears.

Through music, melody and rhythm find their way

into the secret places of the soul, radiating joy.

Nothing costs so little as a few words of recognition.

Responsibility toward one's fellowmen
is the very essence of social living, and it is, in no
small measure, responsible for what business
success most of us achieve.

All growth must come from inside – by starting
with yourself, you should realize that within you,
you have the germ of goodness, based upon
faith in Almighty God.

As long as a people or nation puts its trust in God, that people or nation will always be happy. That nation is rich in depth, width, and height of strong character and strong citizenship.

Pray, for prayer can work miracles.

We are not created for time but for eternity.

CREDITS

Editing: Barbara Lonnborg

Production: Lisa Pelto

Design: Sacco & Schuster

Photos: Boys Town Hall of History Archives